13582522

Start-Off Stories

KING MIDAS
AND HIS GOLD

By Patricia and Fredrick McKissack

Illustrated by Tom Dunnington

Prepared under the direction of Robert Hillerich, Ph.D.

CHILDRENS PRESS ®

CHICAGO

Library of Congress Cataloging-in-Publication Data

McKissack, Pat, 1944—
  King Midas and his gold.

  (Start-off stories)
  Summary: King Midas discovers that gold does not make him happy after all, especially when he can't eat it or love it.
  1. Midas—Juvenile literature. [1. Midas.
2. Mythology, Greek] I. Midas. II. Title.
BL820.M55M34 1986   398.2'2   86-11744
ISBN 0-516-03984-9

WM
J
398.22
Mck
7.25

Midas was a king.
But he was not happy.
"I wish for gold," he said.
"Gold will make me happy."

Ping! He got his wish.

King Midas saw
an apple.
Ping!
It was gold.

A cup.
Ping!
It was gold.

A box.
Ping!
It was gold, too.

King Midas was happy.
He had gold, gold, gold.

King Midas saw a rose.

"Oh, pretty rose."

Ping!

The rose was gold.

King Midas did not like that.

King Midas saw his dog.
"Oh, good dog."

Ping!

The dog was gold.

King Midas did not like that.

King Midas was king.
But he was not very happy.
He could not eat.

He could not sleep.

He could not do much.
Ping! Ping! Ping!

17

Ping!
The cook was gold.

Ping!
The queen was gold.

"No. No.
Go. Go.
Oh, no!"

Ping!
The princess was gold!

24

All he had was gold, gold, gold!
King Midas did not like that.

"I wish there was no
more gold," he said.
And he got his wish.

Ping!
Back came the princess,
the queen,
the cook,
the dog,

the rose,
the box,
the cup,
and the apple!

King Midas could eat.
He could sleep.

"No more gold," he said.
And this made him happy.

a	dog	king	queen
all	eat	like	rose
an	for	make	said
and	go	me	saw
apple	gold	Midas	sleep
back	good	more	that
box	got	much	the
but	had	no	there
came	happy	not	this
cook	he	oh	too
could	his	ping	was
cup	I	pretty	will
did	it	princess	wish
do			

The vocabulary of *King Midas and His Gold* correlates with the following word lists: Dolch 63%, Hillerich 59%, Durr 67%.

About the Authors

Patricia and Fredrick McKissack are freelance writers, editors, and teachers of writing. They are the owners of All-Writing Services, located in Clayton, Missouri. Since 1975, the McKissacks have published numerous magazine articles and stories for juvenile and adult readers. They also have conducted educational and editorial workshops throughout the country. The McKissacks and their three teenage sons live in a large remodeled inner-city home in St. Louis.

About the Artist

Tom Dunnington hails from the Midwest, having lived in Minnesota, Iowa, Illinois, and Indiana. He attended the John Herron Institute of Art in Indianapolis and the American Academy of Art and the Chicago Art Institute in Chicago. He has been an art instructor and illustrator for many years. In addition to illustrating books, Mr. Dunnington is working on a series of paintings of endangered birds (produced as limited edition prints). His current residence is in Oak Park, Illinois, where he works as a free-lance illustrator and is active in church and community youth work.